الله جَلَّ جَلالُه

There is no god but God. In the name of God the Compassionate, the Merciful. And Muhammad ﷺ is His Prophet.

Muhammad ص

محمد رسول الله

written and illustrated by Demi

MARGARET K. MCELDERRY BOOKS ❖ NEW YORK LONDON TORONTO SYDNEY SINGAPORE

IN KEEPING WITH ISLAMIC TRADITION, THE PROPHET MUHAMMAD ﷺ AND HIS FAMILY
HAVE NOT BEEN DEPICTED IN THIS BOOK.

❧

The symbol we used after the Prophet's name is a traditional form of benediction.

FOREWORD

Demi's text and illustrations, based on traditional Islamic sources and artistic expression, express the life of Prophet Muhammad ﷺ in a most beautiful way. Muslims believe that Muhammad ﷺ was a Messenger of God who brought to humankind not a new religion called Islam, but the same message that had been given to all of the prophets of the Old Testament and to Jesus, peace be upon them all. The Arabic word *islam* means "submission to God's will," and this message of submission was the same message that other prophets had given. The Arabic word for God is *al-Lah* or *Allah*, which means "The God." The word *Allah* is used by Arabic-speaking Jews, Christians, and Muslims, much as the word *God* is used by English speakers. The expression "There is no god but God" that appears in Demi's text uses a small "g" for a god that is not The One God and a capital "G" for The One God, who is the basis of worship among monotheists.

The artistic tradition depicted here by Demi is one that is almost unknown to the Western world. In this book there are no specific drawings of the Prophet and his family. This is because the Islamic tradition, like the Jewish tradition, has always followed the ten commandments, in particular, "Thou shalt not create graven images." As a result of following this commandment, Islamic art developed avenues of artistic expression other than the human form, taking numbers and geometry, plant and animal life to their highest form of human expression. This was then enhanced by the presence of the Word of God as revealed in the Koran in the Arabic language through the art of calligraphy. Geometric, arabesque, and calligraphic forms replaced the human form as it is believed that the artistic representation of the human form may lead to the worship of that human-created form instead of the worship of The One God who created everything. However, in regard to depicting angels or people other than the Prophet, Yusuf al-Qaradawi says in *The Lawful and the Prohibited in Islam*, "If someone wants to make a picture of an animate being with no intention of competing with God as Creator or for its glorification or respect, there is no prohibition of doing so; there are numerous sound Traditions (ahadith) in this regard" ([Plainfield, Ind.: American Trust Publications, 1994], 110).

In keeping with this artistic tradition, Demi chose the style of the Persian miniature, which is historically one of the earliest artistic forms of book illustration. It is a style that is conveyed in a two-dimensional format so that the viewer creates the third dimension in his or her mind. The absence of the third dimension and therefore of shadow relates the artwork to the imaginal world where the archetypes of The One God's Names and Qualities reside.

This is the first, long-awaited biography of Prophet Muhammad ﷺ for children in a Western language. It should be translated into all languages to give children all over the world the opportunity to learn of another kind of artistic expression, one that respects the beliefs of the more than one billion people of the world whose fourteen-hundred-year history of artistry has been for the most part forgotten by the modern world.

—Laleh Bakhtiar, Ph.D.
student of Seyyed Hossein Nasr
Chicago, June 2002

Laleh Bakhtiar, Ph.D., was born in Tehran and moved to America as a child. She married and raised a family in Tehran and currently lives in Chicago, Illinois, where she is the president of the Institute of Traditional Psychology. She also works as a translator, editor, and psychotherapist and is the author of more than twenty books on Sufism, including *The Sense of Unity: The Sufi Tradition in Persian Architecture* (with Nader Ardalan), *Sufi Women of America*, and *Sufi Expressions of the Mystic Quest*.

Muhammad ﷺ was born in Mecca in the Arabian Peninsula, in the year 570 A.D., into a powerful and influential tribe, the Bani Hashem. Sadly, Muhammad's ﷺ father died two months before he was born. His grandfather gave him the name Muhammad ﷺ, which means "often praised" or "praiseworthy."

Following the custom of the time, when he was very small Muhammad ﷺ was taken by his mother into the desert to be raised by a nurse. It was believed that growing up in the open air would make a child strong and healthy. So, for the first five years of his life, Muhammad ﷺ was raised by nurse Halima, who recognized in the child an inner beauty and greatness.

As soon as he could walk, Muhammad ﷺ helped the desert shepherds tend their flocks of goats and sheep. He had no formal schooling and could neither read nor write. But Muhammad ﷺ studied and learned from the hardworking people and the natural world surrounding him.

Muhammad's ﷺ mother died when he was six years old, and he was taken in by his grandfather, Abdul Muttalib, who was an elder of Mecca. For two years Muhammad ﷺ sat at his grandfather's side, observing intently as his grandfather gave counsel to the people who came to him for help and advice. Abdul Muttalib loved Muhammad ﷺ dearly and thought he would be a great leader one day.

When Muhammad ﷺ was eight years old, Abdul Muttalib died. The boy found himself in the care of his uncle Abu Talib, who was a merchandise trader. Muhammad ﷺ drove the camels and traveled great distances with his uncle, meeting new people and seeing new places.

It was on a journey to Syria that a Christian hermit named Buheira noticed Abu Talib's caravan. He invited the travelers to join him for a meal and asked about the boy Muhammadﷺ. Buheira told Abu Talib to take special care of Muhammadﷺ, predicting that he would become a great prophet.

Young Muhammad ﷺ grew tall and strong and he was said to possess great beauty, particularly because of his deep-set black eyes and thick beard. He was quiet, wise, and deeply drawn to God, whose Arabic name is Allah. Muhammad ﷺ spent much time thinking about the world around him. He was troubled by how the very rich treated the poor so badly. In business matters, people often cheated one another and did not give a fair share to those who deserved it. Because of his sincerity, sense of fairness, and honesty in conducting business, Muhammad ﷺ was called "al-Amin," which means "the trustworthy." People trusted Muhammad ﷺ so much that they asked him to settle disputes among them.

Muhammad's ﷺ remarkable qualities were noticed by Khadijah, a beautiful, wealthy widow fifteen years his senior. She hired Muhammad ﷺ to work as her agent in trade.

Muhammad ﷺ proved himself so successful, kind, polite, and mature that when he was twenty-five, Khadijah asked him to marry her. Their life together was happy and they were blessed with two sons and four daughters. Muhammad ﷺ and Khadijah were equal partners. They respected each other and always helped one another.

Muhammad ﷺ went often to Mount Hira, just outside Mecca, where he sat for hours in a cave, reflecting and meditating on the mysteries of life. One night in the month of Ramadan, in the year 610, Muhammad ﷺ received a revelation from God, brought by the angel Gabriel. During this "Night of Power," Muhammad ﷺ was called upon to be God's messenger, to make known God's will to the whole of humanity, and to show the way to human dignity, progress, and real happiness.

The angel Gabriel squeezed Muhammad ﷺ tightly.

"Recite," he said to Muhammad ﷺ.

"What should I recite?" Muhammad ﷺ asked.

"Recite!" Gabriel repeated, and for a third time, "Recite!" And under this inspiration Muhammad ﷺ recited: "In the name of the Lord who created. Created the human being from a clot of blood. The Lord is most bounteous who teaches by the pen, who teaches the human being that which he did not know!"

Thus were revealed to Muhammad ﷺ the first verses of the Koran, the eternal and infallible word of God, and the holy book of the religion of Islam.

After these first verses were revealed, Muhammad ﷺ went from the mountain to his wife Khadijah. He was trembling and she held him tightly when he told her what had happened in the cave. She said, "You are a good man; I believe you and trust you."

Khadijah was Muhammad's ﷺ first convert to Islam, and his ten-year-old cousin, Ali, was the second. Abu Bakr, Muhammad's ﷺ closest friend, was the third, and Zaid, a freed slave, was the fourth.

From then on, the voice of Islam rang louder and louder as Muhammad ﷺ proclaimed the message of God, preaching the existence of only one God, the importance of equality for all people, and the necessity of freedom of thought and speech.

The angel Gabriel appeared again and again to Muhammad ﷺ, delivering more and more of the sacred word of God. Muhammad ﷺ memorized the words and had scribes write them down. After twenty-three years, the Koran was complete.

Your God is One God;
There is no God but He;
The All-Merciful, the All-Compassionate.
Behold in the creation
of the Heavens and the earth;
in the alternation
of night and day;
in the sailing of ships
through the ocean
for the profit of mankind;
in the rain which God
sends down from the skies,
and the life He gives therewith
to an earth that is dead;
in the creatures of all kinds
that He causes to multiply
through the earth;
in the change of the winds,
and the clouds which run
their appointed courses
between sky and earth;
in all this are signs indeed
for people who use their reason.

Koran 2:163-164

At this time, the various tribes of Mecca believed in many different gods and worshipped hundreds of idols. Their finest place of worship was the sacred shrine of the Kabah—a square structure with a black meteorite set into the lower eastern corner. It was believed that the meteorite had fallen from Heaven as a sign of the first covenant between God and man.

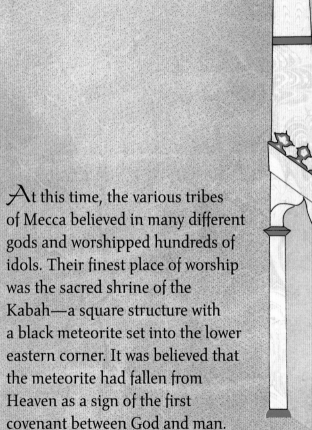

Muhammad ﷺ felt that Quraysh leaders of the Meccan tribes had forgotten the truth behind the first covenant between God and men—that men were supposed to worship not many gods, but only *one* God. But the Quraysh, who had grown rich creating new deities and idols for their people to worship, were not easily convinced by Muhammad's ﷺ proclamations and felt threatened by Islam. They began a persecution of Muhammad's ﷺ followers, some of whom fled to the protection of the Christian king in Ethiopia.

Muhammadﷺ knew the path before him would be hard, but its direction was clear. Muhammadﷺ continued to share the words of the Koran, and over time more and more people joined the Prophet. People accepted Islam because Muhammadﷺ taught God's words that said that all men and women, black and white, rich and poor, must be treated with dignity and respect.

Some of the nobles balked at the idea of treating the weak and unprotected with justice. They challenged Muhammadﷺ to produce miracles if he was a real prophet. "I am only a human being like yourselves," he said. "My miracle is the Koran."

Umar, a fierce and feared tribal leader, charged through the streets of Mecca with his sword drawn, looking for Muhammadﷺ. People retreated in alarm, but one man approached Umar, telling him to go to his sister's house before trying to kill Muhammadﷺ. As soon as he entered his sister's house, Umar heard verses from the Koran being recited. As he listened, his heart softened and the fearless warrior began to cry. He found Muhammadﷺ and accepted Islam.

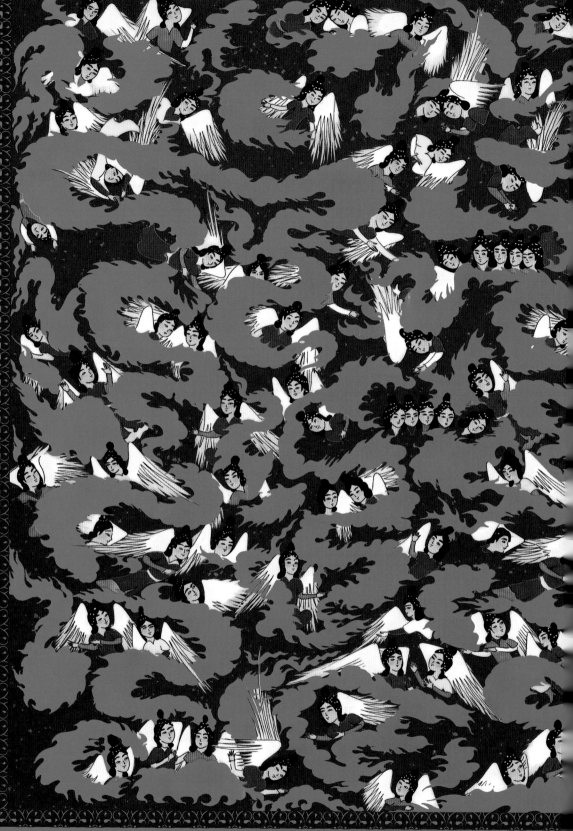

On a night in the year 620, shortly after Khadijah died, Gabriel appeared to Muhammad ﷺ to prepare him for a night journey through paradise that came to be known as the Ascension, or Mi'raj.

Muhammad ﷺ mounted a divine creature called Buraq and rode from Mecca to Jerusalem, where he led the prophets Abraham, Moses, and Jesus in prayer.

Muhammad ص traveled with the angels,
ascending through the heavens, until
he reached the Seventh Heaven where
he was brought into the light of God's
presence himself.

Muhammad ﷺ was shown a window into Heaven and instructed to have his followers make five daily prayers. He then returned to Mecca, where he shared his incredible story with his followers.

The Quraysh leaders continued their efforts to crush Islam by threats, stonings, beatings, and all forms of persecution. They even plotted against Muhammad's ﷺ life.

In the year 622 Muhammad ﷺ received a message from God to leave Mecca and journey to Yathrib, which was renamed Medina, where Islam would be welcomed. Muhammad ﷺ and his followers began their great flight, or Hijra, at night, leaving Mecca on camels, on horses, and by foot. The Quraysh learned of the Hijra and set soldiers upon Muhammad ﷺ with swords. Protected by God from being seen and heard, Muhammad ﷺ managed to escape unharmed.

Later that night Muhammad ﷺ and his friend Abu Bakr hid in a cave. God caused a spider's web to be spun over the entrance to the cave and a dove to make a nest near the cave opening.

When they saw the unbroken spider's web and the dove on her nest, the Quraysh soldiers turned away from the cave. Though they searched far and wide, the soldiers could not find Muhammad ﷺ and Abu Bakr and thus they were saved.

The children of Medina sang a song of welcome from atop palm trees and along the streets. Everyone wished for the Prophet to stay in their home, so, to be fair, Muhammad ﷺ let his camel decide where they would rest. The camel stopped before a humble home belonging to Abu Ayyub Ansari and that is where Muhammad ﷺ stayed. Straight away Muhammad ﷺ began to build the simple mosque of Medina next to which he would live for the rest of his life.

The faithful—the Muslims—were unsure of how to call people to prayer in the new mosque. The Christians used a bell and the Jews blew a ram's horn, but what should Muslims use? A drum was suggested, but Muhammad ﷺ rejected it as too warlike. God inspired him to use the human voice to announce the hour of prayer. The Prophet asked Bilal, a former Abyssinian slave, to call: "Allahu Akbar! ("God is greater!") Allahu Akbar! I bear witness! Allahu Akbar! Allahu Akbar! I bear witness that there is no god but God! I bear witness that Muhammad ﷺ is the Messenger of God! Come to Prayer! Come to Prayer! Come to salvation! Come to salvation! Allahu Akbar! Allahu Akbar! There is no god but God!"

After the Muslims were called to prayer, Muhammad ﷺ mounted the minbar to give his first sermon in Medina. He said, "Every Muslim is a brother of every other Muslim! This is the teaching of Islam!" Because the muhajiroon, or refugees from Mecca, had no belongings, Muhammad ﷺ declared that each Medinite man would give half of whatever he had to a Meccan man, thus creating an inseparable bond of brotherhood.

They are righteous who believe in God . . .
who donate goods and money
for love of God to relatives and orphans,
and to the poor and the wayfarer,
and to the needy . . .
and who are in constant prayer,
and gives alms for welfare,
and those who fulfill their promises
when they make them,
and who are patient
in suffering, adversity and hard times.
They are the truthful ones,
and they are the compassionate.

      —Koran 2:177

In the year 624 Muhammadﷺ, followed by his standard bearers, led three hundred Muslims against one thousand Quraysh raiders in the Battle of Badr, and won more converts to Islam. Believing that their victory was due to God's divine intervention, the Muslims were strengthened. They won the respect of their enemies, and Muhammadﷺ became not only the leader of the Islamic faith but also the head of the state of Islam.

While the Jewish tribe of Banu Quraida lived peacefully in Medina with the Muslims, other Jewish tribes felt threatened by Muhammad ﷺ and the rise of Islam. Jewish agents from Khaibar were sent all over Arabia to unite the local tribes against Islam. In the year 627 ten thousand Arab warriors converged upon Medina in what became known as the Battle of the Trench. Muhammad ﷺ ordered a huge trench to be dug around Medina. The allied tribes could not cross the trench and so laid siege outside the city for twenty-six days. On the twenty-seventh day, a tremendous cyclone struck the allied tribes' camps, thus ending the siege.

Muslims believed God had once again helped Islam prevail, and Muhammad ﷺ sent letters to the kings of Ethiopia, Persia, Yemen, and the Emperor Heraclitus of Byzantium, inviting them to accept Islam.

In the year 628 Muhammad ﷺ led fourteen hundred followers back into Mecca. In the Treaty of Hudaybiyya, Muhammad ﷺ came to a ten-year truce with the Quraysh, who agreed to recognize Muhammad's ﷺ right to proselytize without hindrance and allow him to make a pilgrimage to the Kabah.

So many new converts joined Islam that by January in the year 630, when the Quraysh broke the treaty, Muhammad ﷺ was able to ride into Mecca with ten thousand men and take the city without a fight.

On camelback Muhammad ﷺ circled the Kabah seven times, ordering that all idols be destroyed. He rededicated the Kabah shrine to God and the Islamic call to prayer was soon heard throughout all of Mecca. He met with and forgave even his bitterest enemies, many of whom accepted Islam.

In the year 631, called The Year of Embassies, Muhammad ﷺ succeeded in uniting feuding Arab tribes into a brotherhood called the Ummah. Islam was accepted by the Arabian tribes.

Muhammad ﷺ tried to be a magnanimous victor, setting a model of leniency for all future Islamic conquerors, reminding his followers of the importance of compassion and brotherhood. He granted religious tolerance to Christians and Jewish people who paid a tax, or "tribute." The Biblical prophets from Abraham to Jesus Christ were honored by Islam as prophets and the Jewish Scriptures and the words of Jesus were respected, but the revelations of Muhammad ﷺ, preserved in the Koran, and the Prophet's sayings in less sacred writings called the Sunnah, represented to his followers the final expression of the will of God, who is one being, not a Trinity.

The Koran and the Sunnah became guides that provided a model of ideal moral and social behavior to be followed by every Muslim. True believers were to honor their parents, treat women with kindness, help the poor, protect orphans, and be honorable and just in all personal and professional matters. Followers were to avoid alcohol, pork, and gambling, and be humble before God. Such would enable followers to enjoy the delights of Heaven after their death.

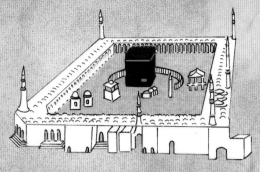

Muhammad ﷺ did not institute an organized priesthood, altars, or sacraments. He prescribed several key observances, which are known as the Five Pillars of Islam:

BEARING WITNESS (SHAHADAH): Muslims declare acceptance of one God— Allah—and Muhammad ﷺ as his prophet.

PRAYER (SALAT): Five times a day—at dawn, noon, late afternoon, sunset, and after nightfall—Muslims face the Kabah in ritual prayer. Ablutions—with sand, if no water is present—precede these devotions. Private prayer, or Du'a, may be said anytime.

ALMSGIVING (ZAKAT): Regular charity purifies man's remaining wealth.

FASTING (SAWM): Muslims go without food from dawn to sunset during the month of Ramadan, thereby purifying the soul and bringing oneself closer to God.

PILGRIMAGE (HAJJ): Every Muslim should make at least one pilgrimage to Mecca. Such a journey joins Muslims from afar, enriches brotherhood and the exchange of ideas.

Muhammad ﷺ preached his final Revelation in the Valley of Arafat, outside Medina, in the year 632. Thousands and thousands of followers were gathered to hear the Prophet. Sitting atop a camel, Muhammad ﷺ recited the final verse of the Koran, saying, "Today I have perfected your faith and completed my blessings on you and chosen Islam as your religion."

"Let there be no compulsion in religion; Truth stands out clear, henceforth, from error."

⸳Koran 2:256

Muhammad ﷺ made a final pilgrimage to Mecca and then returned to Medina. He distributed his worldly possessions to the poor, reminded his followers that the faithful would follow him, and three months later Muhammad ﷺ passed away peacefully.

To the waiting multitude Muhammad's ﷺ great friend Abu Bakr declared, "If you worship Muhammad ﷺ, Muhammad ﷺ is dead. But if you worship God, God is living, eternal and immortal!"

When a person dies,

his deeds come to an end,

except in respect of three matters

which he leaves behind:

a continuing charity,

knowledge from which

benefit can be derived, and

righteous children

who will pray for him.

— Prophet Muhammad

Lā ilāha illa 'Llāh!

These four Arabic words that mean "There is no god but God" are the essence and seed of Islam, the youngest of humanity's great universal religions, which is currently practiced by over one billion people, or nearly one-quarter of the world's population.

Islam honors a single, all powerful, merciful God—Allah. God has many attributes, including the Kindest, the most Loving, and the most Giving. The attributes most mentioned in the Koran are *Rahman* and *Rahim*—the All-Merciful and the All-Compassionate. Muslims utter these two words in all of their prayers and before they begin any task. These attributes remind Muslims that God is merciful to all creation, no matter how small, how insignificant, and that his compassion is everlasting for all of humankind. God is the beginning and the end of all creation, and by speaking the phrase, "There is no god but God and Muhammad ﷺ is the Messenger of God" (*"Lā ilāha illa'Llāh, Muhammadan rasul Allah"*), one becomes a Muslim.

Bibliography

TEXT REFERENCES

Al-Bukhari, Sahih. *Hadith.* Translated by Dr. Muhammad Muhsin Khan. Medina Al-Munawwara: Islamic University.

Asad, Muhammad. *The Message of the Qur'an.* Gibraltar: Dar Al-Andalus, 1964.

Haykal, Husein. *The Life of Muhammad*ﷺ. Translated by Isma'il Raji al-Faruqi. Kuala Lumpur, Malaysia: Islamic Book Trust, 1976.

Lings, Martin. *Muhammad*ﷺ. Rochester, Vermont: Inner Traditions International, 1983.

Nasr, Seyyed Hossein. *Islamic Art and Spirituality.* New York: State University of New York Press, 1987.

ART REFERENCES

Allegrone, Kathleen H. *Patterns and Precisions: The Arts and Sciences of Islam.* Booklet produced to accompany the exhibition "The Heritage of Islam." National Committee to Honor the 14th Centennial of Islam, 1982.

And, Metin. *Minyaturlerle Osmanli-Islam Mitologyasi.* Istanbul: Akbank, 1998.

Stewart, Desmond, and Time-Life Books editors. *Early Islam: Great Ages of Man.* New York: Time, Inc., 1967.

Welch, Stuart Cary, editor. *Treasures of Islam.* London: Sotheby's/Philip Wilson Publishers, 1985.

Nameh, Miraj. *The Miraculous Journey of Mahomet*ﷺ. Paris: George Braziller, 1977.

THE AUTHOR AND EDITOR WISH TO THANK AFEEFA SYEED,

CODIRECTOR OF THE MUSLIM EDUCATION RESOURCE COUNCIL, INC.,

FOR HER INVALUABLE ASSISTANCE IN THE PREPARATION

OF THE TEXT FOR THIS BOOK.

❖

*For all in one
And one in all*

❖

Margaret K. McElderry Books   An imprint of Simon & Schuster Children's Publishing Division
1230 Avenue of the Americas, New York, New York 10020   Copyright © 2003 by Demi   All rights
reserved, including the right of reproduction in whole or in part in any form.   The text for this book
is set in Gilgamesh.   The illustrations for this book are rendered in paint and ink.   Title calligraphy by
Jeanyee Wong   Map by Rick Britton   Manufactured in China
2   4   6   8   10   9   7   5   3   1
LIBRARY OF CONGRESS CATALOGING-IN-PUBLICATION DATA Demi. Muhammad ﷺ / Demi ; foreword written
by Laleh Bakhtiar.— 1st ed. p. cm. Includes bibliographical references. Summary: Introduces
Muhammad ﷺ and the basic tenets of the Islamic faith. ISBN 0-689-85264-9 (hardcover) 1. Muòhammad, Prophet, d. 632—Juvenile literature. 2. Muslims—Saudi Arabia—Biography—Juvenile literature.
[1. Muòhammad, Prophet, d. 632 2. Prophets. 3. Islam—Customs and practices.]
I. Title. BP75 .D37 2003 297.6'3—dc21 2002002985

FIRST
EDITION